CAMBUS BUS MEMORIES in Colour

By Andrew Bartlett

Copyright IRWELL PRESS Ltd.,
ISBN 978-1-906919-72-6
First published in 2014 by Irwell Press Ltd., 59A, High
Street, Clophill, Bedfordshire, MK45 4BE
Printed by 1010, China.

Eastern Counties was one of several large companies that the government decreed should be split up prior to privatisation and on 9 September 1984, its western area operations went to a new company. Cambus Ltd inherited 172 vehicles, of which, not surprisingly, given the Tilling Group background, 128 were Bristols. Where I had come from, only Leicester City Transport had ever operated Bristol products (and then not many of them). There were depots at Cambridge, Peterborough, Ely, March, and Newmarket (actually in Suffolk), and stage carriage services were operated throughout Cambridgeshire and into neighbouring counties; Spalding and The Deepings in Lincolnshire, King's Lynn in Norfolk, Haverhill and Mildenhall in Suffolk, Saffron Walden in Essex, Royston in Hertfordshire and Oundle in Northamptonshire. More National Express and tour work came at the end of November 1985 from Ambassador Travel, the other offshoot of Eastern Counties, along with 24 vehicles.

Having taken on a new job in London, I moved to St Ives – the one in Cambridgeshire – in May 1985 and assumed the life of a long-distance commuter. On my first morning, what should greet me on the 132 service to Huntingdon railway station but Cambus VR 746, in its unmistakeable 'Redline' livery. From such beginnings, trips to other parts of the county indicated that this was a company with an interesting mixture of city and country operations. With camera at the ready, I began to explore.

On 5 December 1985 Cambus became the seventh constituent of the National Bus Company (NBC) to be privatised when it was acquired by its management. The photographs, all except one of which were taken by me, are presented in chronological order of key events: firstly the inherited fleet (1984-86) and the early days of privatisation and deregulation (1986-89); then the formation of Viscount Bus & Coach Co. and the acquisition of Premier Travel Services, and finally Cambus again in the years 1990-95, including further purchases in the form of Millers and Milton Keynes City Bus. The CHL Group, as it was by then, became part of the Stagecoach empire in December 1995 and I have taken that as an appropriate place to end this thirtieth anniversary trip down memory lane as by that time I had returned to live in Leicestershire.

In telling this story, I have recalled the drivers on my commuter service passing on information about vehicles and liveries, to such a degree that one once told me that I knew more about the company than he did – knowledge that I hope I am now putting to good use. Thanks go to my wife Debbie, for her patience and support, my uncomplaining children James and Katie, who often accompanied me on these photographic missions, Claudia Natteri, for her invaluable help with the presentation of the photos, Chris and George at Irwell Press for the opportunity to tell the Cambus story, Paul Roberts who took a look at the proof and the drivers, who answered my questions with endless good grace and were happy for me to photograph them as they went about their work.
Andrew Bartlett, Kibworth Beauchamp, 2014

I didn't mind the light blue livery that Cambus adopted in 1984; no, honestly, I really believed that after the monotony of NBC red and green, it made a refreshing change. It couldn't be denied that it was an appropriate choice for the operating area, but it is also true that in bad weather, it looked pretty dreadful. Here, one of the earliest repaints, RELL 154 (GCL 345N), still appeared smart a year later as it loaded in Peterborough's Queensgate bus station for local service 12A to Werrington on 28 September 1985.

Eastern Counties had ten ECW-bodied Bristol LH6Ls before the split; only two went to Cambus, WEX 924/26S, which were juxtaposed in the new numbering system, becoming 81 and 80 respectively. Allocated to Newmarket, they were regularly used on stage carriage services but could also be seen working staff shuttles between Drummer Street bus station and Cowley Road depot in Cambridge, on which duty 81 was employed on 26 October 1985. Behind it is Series 3 VR 744 (VEX 296X) in 'Camglaze' advertising livery, preparing to depart on the 118 to Gamlingay. At this point 81 was allocated to Ely, but by early 1986, both 80 and 81 had found their way to Cowley Road. They were withdrawn in March 1987 and gained new employment in the north east with Trimdon Motor Services, but any thoughts that the type was finished in Cambridgeshire were dispelled when a single example, 65, was acquired in 1992.

Some of the vehicles acquired from Eastern Counties saw little or no service with Cambus. Instead of having them clutter up the limited space at Hills Road (or indeed the new depot at Cowley Road from August 1985 onwards), these withdrawals were stored at the rear of the Cambridge Road depot in Ely. Most still carried their Eastern Counties fleet numbers, even though on paper at least Cambus numbers had been allocated. On a freezing January day in 1986, the line-up comprised five RELL6Gs, a VR that was new to Central SMT and an FLF6G. This was FLF453, now Cambus 61 (JAH 553D); its semi-derelict state did not last long, as we will see later. Next to it was RL711, Cambus 104 (VAH 711H), whose previous duty had been as an in-garage office at Hills Road. Six of these flat-screen RELLs were in stock, but only three – 102, 103 and 105 – were ever used to any degree.

Here is flat-screen RELL 102 (RAH 681F), photographed in Ely on 28 April 1986 just a couple of months after a surprise repaint into fleet livery received just short of its eighteenth birthday. It wasn't the most comfortable or quiet bus on which to travel, as I discovered on a 109 journey between Ely and Cambridge that day. Originally based at Newmarket, 102 moved to Cambridge in November 1985, where it was often used on the 40 mile round trip to Littleport. It remained at Cowley Road for a further seven years, during which time it received the next livery update, although it was eventually relegated to city services and Park & Ride duties in the main. When Cambus acquired the Milton Keynes Citybus and Buckinghamshire Road Car operations, it was despatched there, receiving fleet number 681. It is still extant, beautifully restored to NBC red livery with Eastern Counties fleetnames and its original fleet number, RL681.

Apart from the 24 RELLs (numbered 100-123), Cambus had a further eight RELHs that had been accorded dual-purpose status owing to their ECW bus bodies being fitted with 49 coach seats. New in 1974, they wore National Express livery as late as 1982, and indeed, after the move, when they became Cambus 151-158, some could still be seen on the company's share of the 797-799 group of routes. Upon repaint, they were given a 'semi coach' scheme of light blue with cream waistband and roof, although there were variations – 154, pictured earlier, in bus livery, and 155, which for a time sported 'Blueline' colours. However, prior to its trip to the paint shop, 152 (GCL 343N) carried 'Redline' livery, and was loading in Drummer Street for Saffron Walden on service 112 on 30 August 1985. The inadequacies of the bus station layout can be clearly seen – it would be closed for rebuilding in April 1986.

36 Leyland Nationals were transferred to Cambus, including some of the oldest still in service with Eastern Counties, and were numbered in the 200 range. Every depot except Newmarket had at least one of the type. March, whose vehicles could be seen in service in Wisbech and Kings Lynn, and as a consequence of which, sometimes as far away as Swaffham or Hunstanton, had two allocated there in September 1984. But major revisions at the end of 1985 left Cambus with just a few Tuesday market day services to King's Lynn and the 336 Peterborough to King's Lynn was curtailed at Wisbech, Eastern Counties assuming responsibility for the remaining section, which was initially numbered 36, then 46. On 24 July 1986, 201 (OAH 551M), which had worked in from Peterborough on the 336, was inbetween duties on the Wisbech town service when I photographed it in the bus station alongside an unidentified RELL.

Back to Cambridge and Drummer Street on 30 August 1985, and Leyland National 2 303 (PEX 619W) had recently arrived on the 114 from Newmarket – one of several different routes between the two centres. New in 1980, and still looking smart in NBC red livery, 303 was one of the eight National 2's that passed to Cambus, five of them (300-303, 307) allocated to Cambridge, the others to Peterborough. They were often seen on the longer stage carriage services, and on at least one occasion, the 799 to London Victoria – scarcely a comfortable journey in a bus-seated vehicle, but doubtless preferable to an RE! 303 was to remain at Cambridge until 1994, spending a couple of years in the Millerbus fleet before it was despatched to the Milton Keynes subsidiary. It gained fleet number 2619 during its short time there; it was withdrawn and sold during 1995.

Coaches were numbered in the 400 range, but Cambus only received four from Eastern Counties in the first instance, all Willowbrook 003 bodied Leyland Leopards. They were regular performers on services to London as well as the 'Eastline' 792, which began in 1982 between Cambridge and Ipswich but which was extended in the west to run from Peterborough the following year (an Ipswich – Felixstowe section was added at the same time, though this was withdrawn in November 1986). Prior to December 1985, Eastern Counties, then Ambassador Travel, operated the 792 jointly with Premier Travel Services; Cambus continued the arrangement throughout the rest of the 1980s. On 19 June 1987 Newmarket resident 400 (JCL 810V), looking a little down-at-heel, was photographed at the Old Cattle Market bus station in Ipswich, having just worked in from Peterborough.

Having originally decided that Eastern Counties coaching operations should be handled by a new subsidiary company, Ambassador Travel, from September 1984, the NBC decreed only a year later that coach work from the depots in Peterborough, Cambridge and Newmarket should move to Cambus, and this took effect on 1 December 1985. In all, 24 vehicles were involved; two were Plaxton bodied Leyland Tigers that became 450 and 451, while the remainder were Leyland Leopards with either Plaxton, Duple or ECW bodies, which took fleet numbers between 410 and 436. In National Holidays livery, ECW bodied example 429 (XPW 879X) was waiting in Drummer Street bus station on 30 January 1986 prior to taking up duty on National Express service 098 to London. It still carried its temporary Cambus fleet name, and had not yet had its new fleet number applied, the '9' being the remains of its former identity, LL879.

Service revisions in 1986 saw the end of through working on the X47 between Peterborough and Birmingham, but the remaining Peterborough to Leicester section continued to be shared by Cambus and Midland Fox until 30 July 1987, when Leicester CityBus would operate it on tender. On 18 July 1987 Plaxton bodied Leyland Leopard 410 (RVF 838R) has just left St Margaret's bus station in Leicester, but the driver has pulled in at the entrance to the adjacent Midland Fox Sandacre Street depot (reopened in 1986 as a base for the Fox Cub minibus fleet) and gone inside to seek assistance for what appeared to be a loss of water. 410 was new in 1976 as Eastern Counties LL838; it came to Cambus from Ambassador Travel in December 1985 and was quickly repainted into NBC-style two-tone blue and cream dual-purpose livery. It passed to Viscount in September 1989, but was withdrawn by the end of that year.

The Cambus outstation at St Ives closed at the start of March 1985, vehicles instead being garaged at United Counties Stukeley Road, Huntingdon, depot. On Sundays, five of them would be parked in the yard behind the depot, with the sixth, which operated the Saturday 2300 155 service from Cambridge to Huntingdon, arriving at 0030, on the forecourt. This one normally provided a good photo opportunity, but on 29 September 1985, the chance to record the rear ends of these VRs from the path at the side of the depot proved irresistible, as they represented each of the different VR marques; United Counties Series 3 876, then Cambus Series 1 500 and finally United Counties Series 2 792. 500 (UAH 374G) was the first VR allocated to Cambridge, in June 1969, and received Cambus livery in October 1984. It was already looking somewhat the worse for wear, but would not be withdrawn until July 1986.

Five Series 1 VRs, 500-504, passed to Cambus, but of these, three were vehicles that had come from Scotland in the great VR/FLF swap of 1973. This is the other indigenous example, 501 (UAH 375G), photographed in Emmanuel Street, Cambridge on 30 August 1985, having just arrived from Haverhill on the 113. This extraordinary vehicle, approaching its seventeenth birthday, appeared one sub-zero morning in early 1986 on my commuter service; though not the usual choice for the flagship route, it was the only one of the six at the outstation that the driver on early turn had been able to readily start at 5.15am. I can vouch for the fact that it had a good turn of speed, though the account of it being clocked at 71mph by a police radar speed trap on the A604 south of Cambridge may be apocryphal. It too was withdrawn in July 1986 when the North Devon VRs were acquired

There were considerably more Series 2 VRs; 28 in all, numbered 600-627. Most were new to Eastern Counties, although a couple had started life with Mansfield & District and, along with two others, came to East Anglia from East Midland. The earliest VR2s dated from 1970/71, and not all of these were repainted into Cambus livery, although 603 (XVF 583J) was one of the fortunate ones, being so treated in April 1985. In another picture taken on 30 August 1985, which demonstrates how gridlocked Cambridge city centre used to become (a situation often caused by the sheer volume of buses and coaches loading and offloading in Emmanuel Street and the bus station), it was attempting to negotiate the taxis and other traffic in Drummer Street with a Park & Ride service from Cowley Road. 603 and four other VR2s were replaced by the acquisitions from North Devon.

Cambus needed to augment its double deck fleet almost from the word go. October 1984 saw the arrival of three Series 2 VRs, 628-630, from Hastings & District (new to Maidstone & District), and they were followed in November by two more, 631 and 632, this time from West Riding. 632 (GHL 192L) was seen in Broad Street, March, having returned from Newmarket on the long 116 service. Behind it is the Grade II listed Memorial Fountain, built to commemorate the coronation of King George V and Queen Mary in 1911, and the focal point of the town's bus network. English Heritage describe it as having 'a domed roof of pierced cast iron terminating in finial with lamp. Open sided, with elaborate work to spandrels and capitals of columns.' Originally, it provided water for both humans and animals, but the drinking water fountain was a traffic obstruction, and along with the troughs, was removed many years ago.

Setting out for a day's photography in the Peterborough area on 24 July 1986, my first transport, Leyland National 234 working the 151 service, suffered a smashed windscreen at Alconbury. Returning to Stukeley Road depot, United Counties 969, a Series 2 VR acquired from West Riding in 1984, was provided, and our arrival in Peterborough was a creditable 30 minutes late. An excellent day followed, and one of the best photos came from the realisation of what a good vantage point the second floor of the Queensgate car park made. Of the 56 Series 3 VRs Cambus inherited in 1984, 700-755, Peterborough always had the batch from 731-737, and all of them regularly carried advertising liveries during their Cambus and Viscount lifetimes. Besides this striking example, recently applied to 733 (KVF 246V), and which it carried until 1991, both 747 and 755 also had visually attractive liveries for The Computer Centre at various times.

Cambridgeshire Pick-Me-Up was a service network in the rural area between Huntingdon and Peterborough introduced by Eastern Counties in May 1976. Most were one day a week workings, a notable exception being the Monday-Friday commuter 132 serving Huntingdon railway station. Initially worked by a Ford AO609 based at St Ives, by 1981 something larger was required, and two new VRs from a batch of ten diverted from United Counties, VR303 and VR304, were given 'Redline' white and red livery and put to work on the network. VR304 became Cambus 746 (VEX 304X); it spent a lot of its working life at either Huntingdon or St Ives outstations and was by far my most 'travelled on' bus, but on 11 July 1985 it was on the 186 New Hospital (nowadays known as Addenbrooke's) route in St Andrew's Street, Cambridge, where the driver has temporarily deserted his pal on the bike to collect more fares.

In October 1985, one of the drivers suggested I should visit Ely so as to find, hiding behind the depot, several of the company's first Ford Transits. They had Dormobile conversions and carried a new style of livery – dark blue skirt with a cream band above, upswept at the rear, with light blue above that. They were numbered 2000-2014 and were dispersed to various depots to be prepared for service at around the same time as the next batch – 2015-2029 – arrived in January 1986. Their actual introduction was somewhat drawn out; Peterborough depot was first, when four new routes were launched on 27 April, while Cambridge eventually followed suit on 22 June. As time progressed, mini-networks appeared in Royston, Newmarket and here in Haverhill, where, in this photograph from my collection, 2018 (C318 OFL) is turning into the bus station with an H1 'Hillhoppa' service in the spring of 1988.

The arrival of seven Series 3 VRs from North Devon Red Bus on 1 June 1986 not only brightened up the streets of Cambridge, they also heralded a change of livery, with the dark blue skirt and increased amount of cream as first seen on the Transits now adapted for big bus use. 756-760 had been new to Potteries, while 761 and 762 began their working lives with Western National. Most entered service carrying wrap-round advertisements for businesses in the Barnstaple area, leading me to wonder how many Cantabrigians sought out 'Jungleland' as a result of seeing it on the bus! I had photographed it two days earlier when it was carrying fleet number 762, but by 7 June, it had become 761 (PTT 92R), and was on a North Arbury 185 working in Sidney Street – note that it was pressed into service without a Cambridge destination blind. The revised livery was first seen on 758, which entered service in July.

In the autumn of 1986, in the run-up to major service revisions at the end of October, it was hoped that the remaining vehicles in red livery would soon be withdrawn and the new arrivals (and as many of the existing fleet as possible) painted in the new livery. This placed significant demands on the Cambus paint shop. With the risk of a vehicle shortage in the interim, three Series 2 VRs were hired in from United Counties in Bedford for a 2-3 month period. The oldest of the trio, 762 (VNV 762H), was photographed in Sidney Street on 6 September 1986 on the same stand as 761 in the previous picture, although it is working the 186 Kings Hedges (Buchan Road) service (note that both service 185 and 186, on their return to the city centre, carried on to Addenbrooke's hospital). The loans had ended by Christmas.

Deregulation day – 26 October 1986 – saw considerable changes made to Cambridge services, and Cambus turned to the Freight Rover Sherpa to satisfy a further series of route conversions to minibus operation made from that date. 20 were acquired, numbered 2040-2059, and this is 2052 (D352 KVA), loading in Sidney Street on 'Minishuttle' 6 to Fison Road on 15 June 1987. Note the 'Cambridge & District' vinyls, one of four variations added to vehicles around this time (the others being Peterborough, Newmarket or Fenland & District) and the restyling of the livery with the light blue extended over the bonnet area. The type never really found favour, being described as 'brittle'; surprisingly, four of them – 2046, 2049, 2053 and 2057 – never entered service at all. They were all withdrawn in September 1987, being painted white before disposal, and after testing Optare City Pacer and Iveco Daily demonstrators, it was decided that the former would make the best replacements.

Cambus turned to dealers Kirkby Central at the end of 1986 for a total of 17 Leyland Nationals from the Greater Manchester PTE fleet, all bar one of which were new to Lancashire United. The first examples started to appear in December 1986, but it was well into the following year before deliveries were completed, and all were repainted in the new livery before entering service in Cambridge. Their fully automatic gearboxes were a source of some discomfort in the early days, and it was reported that at least two of the type had been converted to normal semi-automatic transmission. They were numbered 250-266, and were well used on local and longer distance stage carriage work; this is 253 (WBN 476T), seen on 25 May 1991 in Water Lane, Oakington, the outer terminus of the 2. It was withdrawn two months later, passing to Kelvin Central as its 1128.

As well as the 17 Nationals. Kirkby Central also supplied nine former Greater Manchester PTE Leyland Fleetlines (800-808) in early 1987, which were also based at Cambridge. Initially it seemed as though they might be used all over the network; they appeared on the 146 service to Royston, and on 6 March 806 was despatched to Huntingdon, where it worked the 1800 commuter service from Huntingdon station, upon which I had the misfortune to ride. It was seriously underpowered; making an appalling racket, it was taken up the hill between Houghton and St Ives in first gear (a job that a Series 3 VR could happily accomplish in fourth), and the final indignity was that it was too tall to fit inside Huntingdon depot! The type eventually settled down on Cambridge city routes, on which 808 (OBN 508R) was employed on 15 June 1987. They were progressively withdrawn during 1989 and 1990.

West Yorkshire PTE also disposed of quite a few buses at deregulation, and three of them made their way to Cambus via dealer Ensign. They were 503-505, Leyland Olympians with Roe bodywork that were allocated to Peterborough on arrival in April 1987. They were repainted in fleet number order, so 503 (UWW 3X) was more or less fresh from the paint shop when seen in Yaxley on 5 May 1987; there was a minor adjustment to the livery, in that the cream and dark blue areas were no longer swept up at the rear. They moved to Cambridge in 1989, where they were confined to city routes, and all three survived to see in the Stagecoach era. 503 was transferred to Gloucester depot in 2002 and then Torquay in 2003, where it was converted to open-top and numbered 14281, while 505 was still in service with Confidence, Leicester (46) in 2014.

The coach fleet had been augmented in May 1987 by the arrival of two new Leyland Royal Tiger Doyens from Kirkby Central. Initially put to work on excursions, they were eventually given National Express livery, as shown here by 458 (D458 EEG), recently arrived from London in Peterborough on 2 January 1988 and about to return to Lincoln Road depot. However, all was not well with the pair, it being said that they were not up to the demands Cambus coaching duties placed upon them, and they were withdrawn after the end of the National Express summer 1988 timetable, being replaced by two of the second-hand Volvo B10Ms. 457 went back to Kirkby in March 1989 when a new Volvo B10M/Plaxton (325) was received, and 458, which had also gone by that time, was later traced to Bridgetime, Cwmbran, re-registered PBZ 1534, and in 2010, to Cwmbran RFC.

The first of the two West Riding VR2s, 631, was taken out of service at Peterborough in April 1987 and converted to open-top layout. Renumbered 70 (GHL 191L) and repainted in two-tone blue and cream local coach livery, it was reallocated to Cambridge (since Peterborough already had an open-top vehicle in the shape of 60, the former FLF452), where it worked local services including Park & Ride whenever the temperamental English summer weather allowed, and even took turns on the Cherry Hinton Folk Festival specials. On 28 May 1989, with little or no fanfare, it appeared with 'City Bus Tour' vinyls for a route around Cambridge that largely mirrored the existing Guide Friday tourist offering. Photographed under threatening skies at the railway station on 1 July 1989, it attracted very little patronage on this occasion – and apparently on many others too, as the service was quietly withdrawn not long after.

By the autumn of 1987 the RELL was an endangered species, with only five examples left from the once 24-strong fleet. It was all the more surprising then to discover that 120 (EPW 516K) had been given the latest livery. The picture, taken on 27 December 1987, shows how well the ECW body looked in the new colours and painting the wheel hubs dark blue to match the skirt added to the overall smartness of a vehicle which was, after all, almost sixteen years old. 120 was the sole resident of the Ramsey outstation, situated in the quaintly named Owls End, a function it fulfilled until the formation of Viscount in September 1989, when, renumbered B3, it was quietly shunted into the reserve fleet. However, it survives in preservation, restored to Eastern Counties livery and with its original RL516 fleet number, in the same ownership as 102.

With the Freight Rover Sherpas gone, Cambus prepared to put their new 25-seat Optare City Pacers into service. The first seven appeared in December 1987, and over the course of the next three months 11 more were added to the fleet, the entire batch taking fleet numbers 900-917. They were eventually allocated 901-912 to Cambridge and 900, 913-917 to Peterborough – appropriately, the final five were registered E913-917 NEW. With their superior acceleration and popular with drivers and passengers alike, they were even accorded their own article in the Cambridge Evening News, headlined 'Cambus Goes For Style', which was no doubt pleasing to management. Photographed from the top of an open-top bus, this is 906 (E906 LVE), making its way along Chesterton Road in Cambridge on the Fison Road service, by now numbered 3A, on 14 November 1992. The last examples of the type left the fleet in 1996.

Cambus acquired ten additional Volvo B10M/Plaxton coaches during 1988. One, 315, was new for continental and extended tour work; the remainder, acquired second-hand, comprised three from Parks of Hamilton (322-324) in December 1988 for Peterborough, and six from Clarkes of London, received the previous January. Numbered 316-321, they were allocated equally between Cambridge and Peterborough and painted in National Express livery, displacing the unfortunate Royal Tiger Doyens and five newer coaches (452-456) which were to be redeployed on the ever-increasing tour work. This is 319 (A519 NCL), its white livery standing out against the stonework of Emmanuel College as it prepares to leave Drummer Street bus station on 8 March 1989 on the X2. It is rare to see company advertising on coaches used for National Express work, so one wonders what National Express, whose regulations applying to coaches used on their services were quite stringent, made of the 'Cambus Leisure Travel' inscription.

March 1988 saw the appearance of three handsome Leyland Olympians with Optare coach bodies in dual-purpose livery, carpeted throughout and capable of seating 70 people. In their early days, 500-502 would be found on the 797 or 798 services to London, or on private hire work. In 1989 502 made its way to Peterborough, where it will be seen later in Viscount ownership, and with the passage of time the Cambridge pair could increasingly be found on longer distance bus work, 501 becoming a Haverhill regular. By the mid-1990s, 500 and 501 were repainted in what was basically bus livery with DP-style stripes. They were reunited with 502 at Cambridge under Stagecoach management, and lasted for six years there before being transferred to Gloucester (500 and 501) and Stroud (502) in 2002. But this is 500 (E500 LFL) when only seven months old, leaving Drummer Street for London on 29 October 1988.

Cambus took the opportunity to acquire ten more Optare City Pacers in 1988. First to arrive were former demonstrators 898 and 899 in the spring. Then in September, 920-927 came from the defunct Taff-Ely fleet, 926 and 927 via National Welsh, all just a year old. Two were allocated to Newmarket, where, appropriately, they became 'Colts', and this is 927 (E750 VWT), working town service N2 in The Rookery on 21 July 1990. Of the remainder, 920 and 921 went to Peterborough, while 922-924 became the first Cambus vehicles to receive a dedicated livery for the service linking Cambridge city centre with the railway station, inconveniently situated a mile away. At first, this was simply Taff-Ely livery with City Rail Link logos, but at the end of 1991, a new version, similar to fleet colours but with maroon replacing the dark blue areas, was introduced. 927 was one of the last City Pacers in service, being withdrawn in late 1996.

Prior to 1986, Delaine services between Peterborough and Bourne via The Deepings ran on the hour and Cambus route 312 worked to Deeping St James on the half-hour. However, after deregulation Delaine started a competing service at XX30 to Deeping St James, and beat Cambus by operating via Bourges Boulevard instead of Lincoln Road. In October 1988 Cambus retaliated, replacing the 312 during the day on weekdays with the D1, which now left Peterborough on the hour and used Bourges Boulevard, thereby cutting 15 minutes off the journey time – hence the route being named 'Timesaver'. National 2 305 (PEX 621W) was dedicated to the D1, and was given this pleasing adaptation of fleet livery, although management's hopes that one vehicle could now work the service were highly optimistic once peak time congestion was encountered. 305 was photographed in poor weather at the Queensgate bus station on 25 November 1988.

Those who hoped that the fleet would be further updated following the arrival of the three Optare bodied Olympians were not to be disappointed when news came of an order for 13 more, this time with Northern Counties 75 seat bodies for bus work. They arrived between December 1988 and March 1989 and initial allocations were 506-511 at Peterborough, 512-515 at Cambridge, 516 at Ely and 517 at Newmarket. This is 507 (F507 NJE), which on 2 September 1989 was most unusually engaged on the S3 Stamford Shuttle service, a network taken over in March 1988 when Barton pulled out of the town, and despite competition from both Kimes and Bland's. But a closer look at the date – just eight days before the Peterborough area operations were to transfer to Viscount – might well be the reason why other vehicles (which were being prepared for the launch) were unavailable.

Brightening up the fleet and bringing in valuable additional revenue, at the beginning of 1989 no fewer than 14 full-size vehicles – one National, the remainder Series 3 VRs – carried advertising liveries, all bar two for a variety of local businesses. The exceptions were 731 and 740, which publicised services provided by Cambus itself. 731, based at Peterborough, carried a dark blue scheme for 'Square Deal Breaks' coaching holidays. Then in July 1989, Cambridge's 740 (RAH 265W), which had been promoting Hereward Radio, appeared in this lime green and pink scheme for 'Camcards' and 'Outbacks', two of the company's range of value tickets. If the plan was for 740 to be noticed, it worked; drivers at St Ives outstation (which had replaced Huntingdon in May 1989) nicknamed it 'the Battenberg', and with good reason! It was working a 155 service from St Ives when seen in Bar Hill on 11 March 1991.

It came as something of a surprise in May 1989 to learn that the northern area operations were to be split off to a new company within Cambus Holdings Ltd. Viscount Bus & Coach Co Ltd was launched with Paul Cooper as managing director on Sunday 10 September 1989, from the depots at Peterborough and March. A new livery of yellow and white with blue and grey stripes was introduced, carried by over 20 vehicles from day one, along with a new fleet numbering system prefixed by B for buses, S (Shuttle) for mini- and midibuses, and T (Travel) for coaches. Four new Optare Star Riders were acquired, and I got up early on that first morning to drive over to Peterborough and photograph S3 (G803 OVA) at the entrance to Lincoln Road depot, as it became the first Viscount to take up duty, on service 52 to Yaxley.

By virtue of its coach seating, Optare bodied Olympian 502 was originally numbered T12, but by May 1990, after the Viscount coach fleet had transferred to Premier Travel, it become B2, and lost its Cambus livery, initially for this all white scheme. It was on the National Express stand at Queensgate bus station on a Bank Holiday Saturday, 26 May 1990, prior to setting out for Skegness on the 470 service, with a large crowd waiting to board. B2 (E502 LFL) did not revisit the paint shop until much later in the year, when it was given standard Viscount bus livery but with vinyls on the front between decks advertising the X65 Peterborough – Oundle – Corby – Kettering – Northampton service on which it was usually found. It kept its coach seating, and was thus suitable for private hire work, and was therefore able to retain Viscount Travel logos.

Market Deeping is an old market town across the Cambridgeshire border in South Kesteven, Lincolnshire, about 10 miles from Peterborough. Eastern Counties established a small depot in nearby Deeping St James, which passed to Cambus and subsequently to Viscount. The allocation was only ever small, but the numbers there would often be swelled by de-licensed vehicles. Olympian B7, named 'Viscount Deeping', was the usual outstation vehicle, but on 23 February 1991, B10 (F510 NJE), was doing the honours when photographed while waiting in the picturesque Market Place in Market Deeping before its return to Peterborough on the D1. The dedicated livery for this service seen earlier adorning 305 ended less than a year after it was introduced, when the two National 2's remaining at Peterborough received Viscount livery in August (304/B20) and November (305/B21) 1989 respectively. In 2014 services to the Deepings are still provided by both Delaine of Bourne (101 and 102) and Stagecoach in Peterborough (12).

Significant anniversaries of two of the companies that went to form Eastern Counties in 1931 were celebrated by Cambus in the late 1980s. In 1987, VR 746 lost its 'Redline' livery for the green of the Ortona Motor Co Ltd of Cambridge, marking 80 years since it was founded; the Cambridge Omnibus Society organised an excellent tour on 2 August 1987 when 746 revisited several former Ortona routes. The following year, it was Peterborough's turn to honour the 85th anniversary of the Peterborough Electric Traction Co Ltd, and VR 737 was chosen to carry the brown lake and cream livery with gold lettering and lining, in which it looked quite superb. It retained the livery into Viscount ownership; here it is as B50 (KVF 250V) leaving Queensgate bus station for Huntingdon on 27 June 1992. In 1993 it was repainted with minor changes to the wording for the 90th anniversary celebration.

Last seen in semi-derelict condition at Ely in January 1986, FLF 61 re-appeared from the Peterborough paint shop in May 1988, beautifully restored in Tilling red and cream livery. It attended various rallies and a Cambus Vintage Bus running day during the first year of its new life, and passed to Viscount in September 1989, taking its old fleet number, FLF453 (JAH 553D), and the name 'Old Scarlett'. From April 1991, it was used for new services from four Peterborough suburbs to Queensgate bus station between 0910 and 1245 on Mondays to Fridays offering special low fares and the services of a conductor. The children and I sampled the FLF in action on 28 May, and I got this picture at Gunthorpe (Harrier); watching the conductor change the blinds was a welcome reminder of the days before one person operation became the norm. Sadly, the routes were discontinued before the year end and did not reappear in 1992.

Cambus ended up with 40 Ford Transits (a later batch of nine with Carlyle bodies and dual-purpose seating – 2031-2039 – being received in July 1986), of which Viscount took 17. No less than 13 of these were taken out of service before the company was launched and given the new livery, and of these, three were given a slightly revised scheme to allow them to carry promotional vinyls, the company never being slow to advertise its own services – in this case discount tickets. S30 was colour-coded green for Fare Savers; S31 was red for City Saver tickets, and S32 blue for the Scholar Saver. S30 (C900 LEW) was leaving Queensgate bus station on its way to Park Farm on Minishuttle route B on 19 June 1990. Ten of the type, including S30-S32, were still in service in the summer of 1993, but they had all been withdrawn by the year end.

The Viscount coaching fleet initially comprised 24 vehicles numbered between T1 and T25 (there was no T16). By virtue of their coach seating, even two of the double deck fleet were included, along with several older vehicles that were withdrawn almost straight away. The newest arrival was T25 (F325 DCL), acquired in April 1989, whose time in Cambus livery was short-lived as by September it had been repainted in this attractive 'Viscount Travel' scheme, a pleasing variation of the style used on the company's buses. It also heralded the practice of naming members of the coach fleet, becoming 'Valiant'. Used on longer distance coach tours in the UK and Europe, I saw it at Queensgate on 10 February 1990. It passed to Premier Travel in May 1990, where it took fleet number 388 and, in due course, received its third livery in as many years. It was eventually withdrawn in April 1994.

Somewhat surprising was the arrival in May 1990 of 27 Series 3 VRs, between 9-11 years old, from West Yorkshire (York City & District) and Keighley & District. Cambus took eight, numbered 730-737 (taking the gap conveniently left by the departing Viscount vehicles six months earlier), while Viscount had no less than 19, B39, B40 and B64-B80. Management hopes that Viscount would become 'the Marks & Spencer of the bus and coach business' were not helped by the length of time it took for them to receive fleet livery – 18 months in some cases, by which time those still waiting were starting to look pretty scruffy. This is one of the former Keighley examples, B74 (SUB 790W), photographed in Westgate on 30 March 1991 as it returned to Peterborough from Spalding. The band between decks, a Keighley feature which appears to be grey in colour, was actually known as chinchilla.

Queensgate bus station, Peterborough, on 19 August 1992, and former York & District VR B66 (LWU 466V), in common with the rest of the Viscount fleet, is carrying a 'We match Fen fares' sticker. The Fen in question was Fen Travel, the result of a management buy-out of the former Blands of Stamford business from Midland Fox, based at Ryhall. The initial service, 3, launched on 20 July 1992, was to the Orton Centre; it was soon followed by further routes to The Ortons, Werrington and Bretton, and two services linking Stamford and Peterborough. The fleet, which included two former Cambus Leyland Leopards (405, 407), was augmented by eight Freight Rover Sherpas ex National Welsh, while Viscount hired in several MCW Metroriders from West Midlands Travel to bolster its fleet. The threat ended abruptly on 27 February 1993 when Fen Travel went into liquidation, but the episode marked the end of Viscount's presence in Stamford.

At the same time that the second-hand vehicles from Yorkshire were making their way down the A1, it was announced that Viscount had three new vehicles on order, and these appeared in August 1990 as B3-B5, all-Leyland Olympians. The first two were allocated to Peterborough while B5 (H475 CEG) was despatched to March, where I photographed it outside the depot in Wisbech Road on 23 February 1991. Vehicle naming had spread to several members of the double deck fleet, sometimes as a result of a competition. Local man Owen Palmer had Olympian B8 named after him for suggesting the names for these three, all famous people associated with Peterborough; Sir Henry Royce (B3), 19th century poet John Clare (B4), and Katherine of Aragon (B5). The latter vehicle left Stagecoach East for Yorkshire in 2006, by now numbered 14525, and passed to Centrebus Holdings when Stagecoach sold its Huddersfield depot in 2008.

The results of the tendering round implemented on Sunday 19 May 1991 brought a number of changes for Cambus and Viscount, and one of the corridors most affected was that between Cambridge, Huntingdon and Peterborough, where Monday – Saturday evening work was lost to Myalls of Bassingbourn (who also took some city work and evenings/Sundays to Ely and Littleport) and Midland Fox (Fairtax). Sunday services were retained, but minibuses became the order of the day. On that first Sunday, Cambus used Optare City Pacer 910, and Viscount had S8 (C518 DYM), one of five Iveco Daily 49.10/Robin Hood 21-seaters it had just acquired from London Buses Bexleybus operations. Whether it was the most suitable vehicle for a service of over 40 miles is highly debatable, but, seen in St Ives bus station en route to Cambridge, there are very few passengers around to worry too much about it.

The remaining Viscount midibus acquisitions during 1992-95 were all new vehicles, albeit in relatively small numbers. First in were three Optare Metroriders (S5-S7) in May 1992. There then followed seven Iveco 59.12s with this distinctive Marshall bodywork (S71-S77). I was privileged enough to be allowed inside Lincoln Road depot on 31 October 1992, where the first of them, S71 (K171 CAV), was being prepared for service, the debris on the floor suggesting that various vinyls were in the process of being added. The four Star Riders then departed the fleet early in 1993, to be replaced that summer by three additional Metroriders which took the fleet numbers S1-S3. Then finally, May 1995 saw the arrival of three more Metroriders, S8-S10. At this time, with the ten Metroriders from West Midlands Travel that were still on loan, the small-vehicle fleet was only two less in number than in September 1989.

Cambus Holdings Ltd (CHL) had already had one go at buying Premier Travel Services in 1987, but on that occasion it was sold to AJS Holdings Ltd. Two years later, however, AJS decided to dispose of most of its southern area operations and CHL was on hand once again, the purchase being finalised on 20 May 1990. It was not a complete buy-out; AJS retained four routes, including the 78/79 for Heathrow and Gatwick airports, which passed to a new company, Cambridge Coach Services Ltd. CHL received a mixture of AEC Reliances, Leyland Leopards and Tigers, Volvos (including fourteen new Expressliners) plus fourteen new Expressliners, a Fleetline and a Mercedes L307D. Two Leylands, carrying the final livery used by Premier Travel before the take-over, were sighted in the yard at Wisbech bus station on 9 September 1990; nearest the camera was Leyland Leopard/Plaxton 291 (CJE 455V) and facing the wall, Leyland Tiger/Plaxton 336 (JNM 743Y).

Leyland National 2 304 and 305 had been based at Peterborough since Eastern Counties days, but after both had been repainted into Viscount livery during 1989, they were deemed surplus to requirements when the former York City & District and Keighley & District VRs were taken into stock. So by April 1990 they were back with Cambus, just prior to the Premier Travel Services acquisition. When that had taken place, Premier Travel's bus services, of which there were 25 in all, were operated by vehicles 'on hire', as registration by Cambus did not take effect until July. So there were various unusual workings during the interim, of which this one, of 304 (PEX 620W) in Drummer Street, having regained its original fleet number, in *Viscount* livery with *Cambus* fleetnames on *Premier Travel* service 9 to Hinton on 26 May 1990, was just about as good as it got.

A 'Vintage Bus Running Day' centred on Queensgate in Peterborough on 15 August 1993 presented an opportunity for an unusual 'then and now' photo. Parked up at the northern end of the bus station was preserved Premier Travel 247 (HLP 10C), a handsome, if nonetheless old-fashioned in appearance, AEC Reliance with Harrington bodywork, one of two acquired from Surrey Motors in 1974. Just reversing out of the next door bay on a National Express duty to London, Volvo B10M-61/Plaxton 381 (G381 REG), one of 14 Expressliners new in March 1990. For 20 years, Premier Travel had been faithful to the Reliance for much of its coaching requirements; the first, acquired in 1959, was Burlingham bodied 114, while the last were six Plaxton bodied examples received between September 1978 and March 1979. Five of these were stored when CHL took over, awaiting a decision on their future.

The first new coaches for Cambus had been five Leyland Tiger/Plaxton Paramount 3500 MkII (452-456) in March 1986. After two years on front-line National Express duties, they were given local coach livery and transferred to tours work. 456 was scrapped following an accident in September 1988, but the remaining four moved to Premier Travel in 1990, where they became 395-398. The longest survivor was 398, which was withdrawn in November 1993, but two that had gone prior to that, 395 and 397, rejoined the fleet on extended loan in 1993. This is 397 (C454 OFL) in dealer white livery, pictured leaving Mill Common bus station in Huntingdon for Peterborough on the X51 (not 051) on 15 May 1993. This service linking Peterborough and Cambridge, with a Saturday extension to Newmarket, was withdrawn on Christmas Eve 1993 and replaced by Stagecoach United Counties X51, running Peterborough-Cambridge only.

Imagine the scene – Paris, on a blustery day, 18 April 1993. I'm here with Howard, celebrating the fact that we've been mates for 30 years. We've had to climb the first two stages of the Eiffel Tower because the lifts weren't working, and we can go no further as the final stage is closed to the public. Getting my breath back, I notice a very familiar livery down at ground level, and understandably, my first thought is whether I will get back in time to photograph it. As it turned out, I needn't have worried, because Premier Travel 409 (J409 TEW) – 'Norseman' – on a tour of the French capital, was still standing in the Place Jacques Rueff an hour later! It had been bought new the previous year, and comparison with the earlier photo of Viscount B25 shows how that livery style had been adapted to suit Premier Travel.

The first sightings of the five AEC Reliances that had been in store came in the summer of 1992, when 280 and 281 were discovered at Cowley Road; 281 at least was out in service on the X51 in July before both were delicensed again. The following year, 276-278 emerged, sporting a new livery of cream with blue stripes, while 280 and 281 joined the Millers Coaches fleet, of which more shortly. This is 276 (WEB 406T) about to leave Queensgate bus station, Peterborough on 29 May 1993 with a lightly laden X51 working, although it must be said that its passengers were enjoying a higher standard of comfort than on the VRs that worked the corridor. 276 was the first to go in November 1994, but found a new use, after conversion, as a training bus for CHL's Buckinghamshire Road Car company. The others soldiered on until final withdrawal in late 1995.

An experiment with an alternative local coach livery on Peterborough Leopard 431 at the end of 1988 – two-tone blue, but applied less sympathetically than the version illustrated earlier on 305 – was soon judged to have failed. But in the post-Viscount era Cambus management were seeking a new identity for their remaining coaches, and in February 1990, Leyland Leopard/Plaxton 421 (JVF 821V) appeared in this striking maroon and light blue scheme with 'CamCoach' fleetnames. It was allocated to Royston outstation, where it was photographed on 10 June 1990, for the 146, and later, the ex-Premier Travel 3, Royston to Cambridge services. Hopes that other vehicles might be similarly treated were dashed, ironically, by the acquisition of Premier Travel; transfers and withdrawals meant that Cambus was left with only three other coaches – 316, 417 and 419 – and by the end of the year 421 had been returned to the two-tone blue local coach scheme.

One of the routes operated by St Ives outstation vehicles was the 171 to Ely. Particularly on Saturdays, the opportunity to fit in a tendered service or two would be taken before the return to St Ives, and that gave rise to some very interesting workings. One was the 127 to Mile End, a hamlet to the east of Ely and possibly the smallest place ever to have its own service. There was also the 125 to Pymore, to where the children and I rode with driver Roger Long on a foggy 1 February 1992. This village, with a population of around 350, changed its name back to the earliest recorded spelling, Pymoor (meaning 'flies over bog'), in 1997. Our transport for the day was VR 717 (PVF 353R), which had been B53 in the Viscount fleet but came back to Cambridge in May 1991; its original fleet number was 710.

With hindsight, it is not difficult to see that CHL was storing up problems for itself by continuing to acquire VRs, as the eventual replacement of them would require larger investment in new – and more modern second-hand – vehicles than had been the case. Indeed, by the early part of 1992, Cambus still had 59 (five Series 2, the rest Series 3) and Viscount 39 (all Series 3); a little over 50% of the combined fleets. This latest arrival was a particularly well-travelled example. 763 (YVV 896S) was new to United Counties (896); it was another that transferred to Milton Keynes City Bus (3896) before being sold to Eastern National, and later Thamesway (3212) before operating with Green, Kirkintilloch, whose livery it is carrying. It was received in November 1991; I took this picture at Cowley Road depot on 1 December, and after a repaint, it eventually entered service on 13 January 1992.

Millers Coaches of Foxton had provided a certain amount of competition to Cambus for some years, but that was brought to an end when it was acquired by CHL on 13 February 1992. Millers coaching work was to continue under the aegis of Premier Travel (David Hurry, the Director of Operations, described Millers to me as being 'closely associated with us'). The vehicles carried Millers livery of white, with red and blue stripes swept up towards the rear, and 'Millers of Cambridge' fleetnames, but did not display fleet numbers, which, although allocated, were used for engineering purposes only. On yet another X51 working, in Drummer Street, Cambridge on 22 September 1993, this is Plaxton-bodied Leyland Tiger HSV 195 (new to Premier Travel as C328 PEW), which was transferred to Millers in March 1993. It retained on paper at least the fleet number 328, which it had carried in its Premier Travel days.

Millerbus operations were geared towards tender and contract work, and a livery that was not too far removed from that of Cambus in style, but using red and cream instead, was adopted. A limited fleet replacement saw National 2s 302-306 and VR2s 615 and 619 moving to Millerbus, but only the National 2s were repainted. Millers also had three Leyland Lynxes; 310 and 311 were given the red and cream colours, as was 312, after it had spent a year in local coach livery, in which guise it was often to be found on the X11 Bury St Edmunds service. The type was widely used on Park & Ride duties, for which they received large logos on the body sides; this was the first attempt to create an identity for this type of work, which has been developed so successfully in the years since. 311 (F168 SMT) was pictured at the Cowley Road site on 16 March 1994.

Two of Miller's five Leyland Lynxes had been the subject of an exchange with Metrobus of Orpington in February 1991. Four vehicles came to Cambridgeshire in return, two Fleetlines, more of which shortly, and two Bedford YMT saloons with relatively rare Wadham Stringer bodywork. Both passed to Cambus, where they were numbered 401 and 403, and it is 403 (D23 CTR) seen here on 2 May 1992, having run into a seemingly deserted Drummer Street bus station with a working on the Saturday-only 120 service from Bassingbourn. The fact that both YMTs received Millerbus livery came as something of a surprise, given that they were not a good fit with the rest of the fleet and in consequence were not heavily used. They had disappeared by the time the February 1993 company fleet list was produced; at some time after that they joined the fleet of Coombs of Weston-super-Mare.

The remaining two vehicles received from Metrobus in February 1991 were ex London Leyland Fleetlines DMS2054 and DMS2173. They were both given this rather smart red and grey livery, but when in February 1992 they were due to transfer to Cambus, DMS2054 was delicensed and said to be minus an engine. It never operated for Cambus/Millerbus, and by March 1994 had been sold and converted into a training bus for Cambridge-based S J Research. DMS2173 was given fleet number 613 (OJD 173R), and was briefly put to work on Park & Ride duties, on which it was photographed on 21 March 1992. After a period on loan to JBS Coaches, Bedford, it went into store at Ely, and was still there at the end of 1994, but there are references on the internet suggesting it was later converted to open-top and re-registered BE 4081 in the fleet of New York Apple Tours.

The final acquisition took place in November 1992, and saw Milton Keynes City Bus join what was now the CHL Group. This took CHL outside its normal operating area for the first time, and into difficult territory which, it has been said, was designed with the car rather than the bus in mind. Vehicles were operated under a variety of different names; Milton Keynes City Bus, Buckinghamshire Road Car, County Line and Johnsons, and over 120 vehicles – mainly minibuses – were involved. New liveries were adopted, that for Buckinghamshire Road Car being green and cream applied in Millerbus style. The finishing touches are here being applied to the future 3724 (LOD 724P), a dual-purpose seated Series 3 VR which began life as Western National 1094 but came from Southern National, in the paint shop at Cowley Road depot, Cambridge, on 26 June 1993.

The livery applied to Milton Keynes City Bus vehicles, of red and cream with black window surrounds with the shortened 'Citybus' fleet name, was virtually identical to the Millerbus style in use in Cambridge, so it's not unreasonable to suppose that it was designed to make inter-fleet transfers much easier. That is precisely the fate that befell 3943 (URP 943W), photographed in Wolverton on 29 December 1993 when en route to Bletchley. It was new to United Counties in 1981, and when that company was split up in 1986 it transferred to Milton Keynes City Bus. It moved once again in 1994, where in the combined Cambus/Millerbus fleet it became 739. Despite the huge influx of Volvo Olympians in 1996 after Stagecoach took over, the Bristol VR was not ousted from Cambus fleets until 2000. 739 did not quite stay the course; it was withdrawn the previous year.

January 1993 saw the arrival of arguably the most unusual buses ever to operate in East Anglia. They were a pair of former SMT (Eastern Scottish) Alexander RLC-bodied Leyland Olympians, only four of which were ever produced – the other two being resident in Hong Kong. They received local coach livery and while 506 (B144 GSC) was put to work on the X11 Cambridge – Bury St Edmunds route, replacing former Millers Lynx 312, 507 was sent to the outstation at Mepal (between Ely and Chatteris) for the 124. Their sheer size and general demeanour earned them the nickname 'The Beasts', but they were not overly popular and it came as no surprise to see them withdrawn in July 1995 after only 2½ years service, 506 moving to Regal, Kirkintilloch, in October. But here it is fresh out of the paint shop, at Cowley Road depot on 23 January 1993.

Apart from 17 Optare Metroriders that joined the Cambus fleet in 1992/93, most of the other minibuses at this time were due for renewal. Cambus turned to the Volvo B6 to replace them, and took a total of 14 between September and December 1993 with the distinctive 32-seat Marshall bodywork. Numbered 155-169 (there was no 166 because registration number '666' was not generally available), they were put to work on Oakington and Cherry Hinton services, though it was not long before they were appearing in other parts of the network, Ely and Newmarket in particular. The final three, 167-169, replaced City Pacers on the Rail Link service 1; commendably, despite the increased seating, the service interval was held at every eight minutes. They were given this revised livery of red, white and light blue, and this is 168 (L668 MFL), photographed under another interesting sky at the railway station on 16 March 1994, with no custom in sight.

A forward-thinking initiative funded by Cambridgeshire County Council was the provision of a free shoppers Shuttle Bus operating a circular route from Emmanuel Street around the centre of Cambridge, much of which by this time had been pedestrianised. Two MCW Metroriders were taken on loan from West Midlands Travel, painted in this eye-catching green and yellow livery, and, in a first for the UK as a whole, fitted with Eminox exhaust treatment systems – basically a combined catalytic convertor and particulate trap which significantly reduced diesel engine emissions. Begun towards the end of 1994, the initial trial was deemed to be sufficiently successful for it to be extended until 1996, when the original vehicles were replaced by Optare Metroriders which ran on compressed natural gas (CNG). But on 30 March 1995, this is W002 (D648 NOE), one of the MCW examples, newly arrived in Emmanuel Street and awaiting a change of driver.

1995 saw the arrival of several Olympians – second-hand B12 from Selby & District for Viscount and 481 and 483 from North Devon for Cambus, along with three new Volvo Olympian/Northern Counties Palatine, 518-520. This is 520 (N520 XER) which on 21 September, having run in from Royston, is now bound for a break at Cowley Road. All three vehicles in shot carry what became the final Cambus livery, introduced in 1989, where white replaced the cream areas. Nine weeks after this, on 6 December, it was announced that Stagecoach had acquired the CHL Group for £12.6million. Within months, 52 new Volvo Olympians had been leased, reducing the number of VRs to just 27. The last vehicle to be repainted in Cambus livery was VR 745, one of the two former Cambridgeshire 'Pick-Me-Ups'; the first into Stagecoach stripes was Roe-bodied Olympian 503, marking the start of a new era for Cambus. But that is a story for another time.